S0-BXC-164

EXTENUATING CIRCUMSTANCES

poems by

Charles Halsted

Finishing Line Press
Georgetown, Kentucky

EXTENUATING CIRCUMSTANCES

Copyright © 2019 by Charles Halsted
ISBN 978-1-64662-042-5 First Edition
All rights reserved under International and Pan-American Copyright Conventions.
No part of this book may be reproduced in any manner whatsoever without written
permission from the publisher, except in the case of brief quotations embodied in
critical articles and reviews.

Publisher: Leah Maines
Editor: Christen Kincaid
Cover Photo: Cindy Davis; http://www.cindydavisphotography.com/
Author Photo: Cindy Davis; http://www.cindydavisphotography.com/
Cover Design: Elizabeth Maines McCleavy

Printed in the USA on acid-free paper.
Order online: www.finishinglinepress.com
also available on amazon.com

Author inquiries and mail orders:
Finishing Line Press
P. O. Box 1626
Georgetown, Kentucky 40324
U. S. A.

Table of Contents

I dedicate this book to my wife of thirty-three years, Ann Wyant Halsted, who has constantly encouraged me and shown never-ending confidence in my capabilities.

HOME FRONT

Bombs in the Night

Tar balls on beaches, blackouts every night
meant battles at sea and German subs near shore.
My English schoolboy pen pal was taken from the sights
of bombers sowing terror on the innocents of war.
The man who pumped gas at the Pegasus sign
was arrested, tried, and convicted, a Nazi spy.
Our fathers were gone, my friend's was killed in France,
while mine, a doctor, was safe behind the lines,
sorting the sick from those too scared to fight.
I dreamed of bombs and fires across the fields,
the creatures of nearby woods in frantic flight,
and invented a ritual to shield me from fear,
to assure my father's return, a secret rite
that endured to prevent the return of bombs in the night.

The Shark's Mouth

The gaping rocky mouth of a shark stands guard
at the ragged Eastern edge of our nation. Its orange-
yellow promontory looms high above huge granite
boulders a-jumble along the shore, while the pungent
smell of black seaweed reaches upward from low-
tide rocks. At high tide, an intruder could drown
in its myriad caves and crevasses.

A rampart against raging waves and spray,
every menacing hurricane that hurtles along
the New England coast threatening havoc
on all that stands in its way, its great open maw
reaches far beyond the bluff, ready to swallow
any ship that ventures too close.

It was a bastion against the British when our nation
was forged two hundred forty years before, threatened
again in eighteen-twelve, when privateers sailed out
in defense of our new nation.

Once more, in nineteen forty-four, a small boy
held this citadel his guardian against Nazi submariners
that dared an Atlantic crossing while his father
and uncles fought them on foreign soil.

Home Front '44

Along a northeastern beach, a small boy
gazes over the rolling ocean, extending
from his low-tide sandy bunker to lands
beyond, where World War II rages on.

Black streaks of oil lap at the shore, tell
of lurking undersea monsters, iron-clad
sharks with gaping jaws that cruise nearby
with hidden periscopes to map the shoreline.
Nazi squadrons prepare to wade ashore,
ravage all that stands in their way.

There's still time to erect a fortress of sand
rising higher, pail by pail, that, when dried,
becomes a bastion, its walls reaching upwards
to battlements for sharpshooters to pick off
Nazi soldiers one by one, as each emerges,
bayonet drawn, from the sea.

Too soon the tide turns, creeps up the beach
without pause. Its leading waves lap
relentlessly close to the sandy fortress
until its walls collapse, its battlements
become pitiful shrinking mounds.

How It Was in the War

In nineteen hundred and forty four,
I was only eight years old.
Our Pa was gone over there in the War
taking care of wounded soldiers.
We never knew when it would end
or if he'd ever come home.

Every other day or so, air-raid sirens
would whoop through the air. The coast
was close enough for nightly blackouts.
We knew from tar balls washed up on shore
that Nazi subs were cruising nearby.

We always had plenty of eggs and milk
since our Ma kept chickens and goats.
When passing by the henhouse,
you could hear their soft cluck-clucks
and smell their rancid shit that we used
to fertilize our victory garden. No need
to spend all our rations in grocery stores.

What I remember most from the War
was when it was time for each chicken to go.
The ones who'd stopped laying eggs
were still good enough to be eaten.

Our Ma would grasp a hatchet in one hand,
grab the worn-out bird by the neck,
lay it across a sawn-off stump, cut off
its head with a whack of her axe.

When she put it back on the ground
the headless chicken would pull itself up,
race around in zigzags and circles, spurting
a fountain of blood till it dropped.

The Monster of Darkness

As a child, he was warned not to seek the Googeebocky,
a beast half human, half spider that dwelled in the dark
of the attic closet where the end was inky black.
The door screeched on its hinges, had neither lock nor key.
Whichever child entered no longer would be seen,
swallowed whole with neither trace nor spark
of life, no opportunity to embark
on childhood, of which the monster made a mockery.

As a man, he learned that a cancer had appeared,
the kind that would quickly spread throughout his stark
naked body if not cut out very soon, he was told.
He trusted his surgeon, though frozen stiff with fear,
since he knew he must pass through a tunnel so black
that the monster of darkness could devour him whole.

We Knew Nothing

When I was eight on August the sixth of forty-five
we took turns pulling the church bell rope
in the same town square our ancestors knew.
They'd rung the same bell when World War One was done.
Now the Second was over, my Pa would come home.

We knew nothing of the cost of the mushroom cloud,
of the thousands of civilians killed in an instant.
We knew nothing of the arms race to come,
of the long peace of mutually assured destruction,
of the coming time we would lose our innocence
in Korea, Vietnam, Iraq, Afghanistan.

We'd never dreamed of a presidential fool,
still unborn when we pulled our church rope,
whose world would revolve around each of his whims,
when the nuclear codes would be in his hand.

The Year the Sox Won the Pennant

I was an eight-year-old kid at the end of the War
when Pete, a fly-boy in the Army Air Corps,
was liberated from a Nazi camp for POWs,
came home to marry Ellie, our upstairs boarder.

Pete had grown up in a western Mass town.
A minor league player before the War,
he taught me to hit, run, and catch, took me
to Fenway in Boston to watch his beloved Red Sox.

It was the same ballpark where Babe Ruth
first played, before the remote owners traded
him off to the hated Yankees of New York,
throwing the Sox into decades of doldrums.
(It did not take me long to learn Red Sox lore.)

But then came the day when a new player
was paid to erase all memories of the Babe.
His name was Ted Williams, he grew up in CA,
and his batting averaged .406 in '41.

Though away in the Navy in World War II,
fighting for our country, just like Pete,
Ted came back full force in '46, when
he batted .342, led the legendary Sox
to their first American League pennant
in eighteen years.

It was during that year that Pete and I sat
in Fenway's left-field stands, looking down at
Ted when the other team was at bat.
When the Sox were up, he often got hits, the longest
ever home run in June of that year, confirming
his hero status in my nine-year-old brain.

When our Sox faced the St. Louis Cardinals
in the World Series, my fourth-grade
classmates and I were glued to a squawk box
with a scratchy-voiced announcer when each
school recess rolled around. After game six,
Ted was injured and out, and the Series was tied.

It was back to St. Louis, October fifteenth, game
scores even with two out in the eighth, Cardinals
at bat, when a country boy named Enos Slaughter
made an eighth-inning dash from first base to home
plate, to win the game, take the World Series,
a calamitous day in Red Sox lore. They would
not win it all for fifty-eight years more.

Melting Pot

We were the rich kids who went to private schools
in the New England towns our ancestors founded.
We lived in big houses with lawns running down
to the river that wound past the famed institution
we were destined to attend. The poor immigrant
kids on the other side had names that started
with Mc, Mac, or O', or ended with an i or an o.

One April afternoon, two friends and I, age twelve,
spotted three other boys on the opposite bank.
We shouted epithets, each ethnically matched.
They ran off, reappeared to block our path,
knocked us down, beat out the privileged crap
jammed down our throats since we were born.

Next year, my dad got a job in LA, sprawling
with migrants from over the nation, nearby
countries, or across the Pacific Ocean, who'd lived
in ethnic enclaves for a few generations. I entered
public school with kids of all ethnicities. One friend
was Japanese-American, another Mexican-American.

My first wife was the daughter of immigrant Greeks.
Her father came over at age twenty-three, for the next
fifteen years peddled ice cream, saved earnings,
returned to fetch a Greek village bride. Their
first child won a state scholar award. She and I
met the first day of medical school.

My children are mixed English and Greek, grandchildren
part English, Greek, Portuguese, Irish. We all look
about the same in our family photo.

HOW TO SIP BEER

Evolution Valley

"You can stay overnight at my place," she says,
thirty-five, tight-ass jeans, two shirt buttons undone.

My pack train makes its way along the trail.
Not quite sixteen, I'm the go-to kid from LA
It's the end of summer; next week I go home.
Three months on the job, and I've become
the guy who throws hitches on horses' backs,
leads a packhorse train through mountains
thousands of feet high to utopian valleys.
We wind through switchbacks that hug
the mountainside with a river roiling below.
One hoof off the trail, the pack train would fall—
all six horses, the dudes, and I would plunge down.

Should I go to her bed in San Francisco
or take my chances with teasing teenage
Sirens back home in LA?

At dusk we arrive at a green valley meadow:
a dark forest surrounds it; a gentle stream ripples through;
distant snow-capped peaks glow in the setting sun.
I untie hitches, unload belongings,
hobble the horses to keep them nearby,
make the campfire blaze, prepare canned dinners.
She and the others sleep by the fire.

I make my bed at river's shore,
contemplate virginity and the stars.

How to Sip Beer

Big brother and I, sixteen in fifty-three,
with two other guys and a thirty-six Ford, just right,
drove Boston–LA in three days. We stopped in DC,
where I gazed in awe at martyred Lincoln by moonlight,
then on through the night in the battle-scarred South,
where our Union great-grandpa fought to free the slaves,
arriving next day at the Mississippi's mouth.
At evening we strolled along Bourbon, the street paved
with sin, and entered a strip joint where I was shown
how to sip beer while staring at flesh never seen.
We crossed the southwestern desert nonstop and wind-blown,
the Mojave on razor-thin tires at one-twenty degrees.
Big brother kept me awake my last turn as a pup;
we'd reached California, where I was bound to grow up.

Bourbon Street Awakening

He strolls along Bourbon. It's a warm summer's eve.
Partiers toss trinkets from balconies.
Trumpeters thrust jazz through open doors,
hoping he'll enter to hear them play.

Only sixteen, he's driven nonstop two days
with his older brother and two other guys.
They've stopped for a break, an overnight stay
in this mecca at the Mississippi's mouth.

Halfway along, a barker calls out.
The door's cracked open to a darkened room—
a strip joint. He stops to stare; he's heard
of such places but has never been inside.

Big brother shows how to belly up to the bar,
drink his beer slowly, make it last half an hour.
This is the first drink he's had unshared.
It doesn't matter he's underage—nobody cares.

Up on the bar, she appears fully clothed,
starts to gyrate, undoes buttons and straps.
A background trio grinds out her refrain.
All present fall silent, eyes fixed on her dance.

Her artistry's in her curves and her moves.
When the music stops, she flashes a smile,
scoops clothes from the floor and disappears.
Beer glass now empty, he's no longer a child.

Going Steady

There've been two different wives in my life.
My first marriage lasted twenty-seven years,
the other's still going strong at thirty-three.

They had one thing in common: both wanted to know
"Whatever happened to old What's-Her-Face (WHF)?"
(Notice my care to keep all three nameless).

We were UniHi sweethearts in west LA
during the fifties when full sex was taboo.
In those days it was called "going all the way."

Only bad girls did it with jocks who might boast.
The furthest the good girls would go was to neck,
parked on Mulholland, far over the lights of the city.

Teenage sex with WHF was like amateur wrestling,
tops off in her room, groping and kissing,
always fearful her Mom might show.

When came the time I was ready for college,
she was left behind for her last high school year,
anxious about new girls I'd have for the picking.

Fast forward twenty-five years: well into my first marriage,
we'd moved to northern CA. WHF was a PhD, still in LA.
She and I met now and then at professional meetings.

She was divorced, I married with children.
We decided we'd still be "just friends," though once
we stayed in the same hotel. Nothing happened.

Student Athlete

At seventeen, accepted by my college pick,
I decided I should become a competing athlete.
Over the summer I trained for the cross-country run,
made the fall freshman team, always placed last.

Next spring, I went out for freshman track,
chose the least desired two-mile event.
Eight laps around the quarter-mile oval, I was
often lapped—passed by the guy in the lead.

The end of the term brought the Little Big Meet,
a freshmen event with our main college rival.
I finished the two-mile run without being lapped,
placed third in ten minutes, twenty-eight seconds.

Now I was viewed as one of the jocks.
Earned an emblem of my graduation year,
to proudly wear on my cardinal sweater.
No problem making next spring's varsity team.

The Big Meet took place at the end of the term.
Our main rival had a world-class star,
a guy destined to run in the summer Olympics,
predicted to shatter the two-mile record.

Coach took me aside to say I could run,
"but," he said, "if you start to get lapped,
head to the side and drop out. It'll look
better that way than straggling in last."

After six laps, two to go, far behind
the pack, I heard number one's footsteps
hard on my heels. Once I'd been lapped,
I veered off the track.

Sixty years later, humiliation long
past, my alumnus appeals always
begin: "Dear Student Athlete. . . ."

True Love

Both nineteen, they spent summer school together,
living in his mother's New England house
at the family estate on the shore north of Boston.

A class in logic toughened their minds, as she,
a California girl, exulted in strange surroundings.
He reveled in showing off his favorite childhood places.

He was sure that she was the one through stolen kisses,
deepening rhythms of shared thoughts and feelings,
her fragrance always fresh, her never-touched breasts
hidden behind starched white blouses.

At the end of the term his heart ached as her plane
vanished in the western sky. Back in college with
separate lives, he in his fraternity, she a sorority girl,
his phone calls were never returned.

Her friends said she'd become engaged
to her high school math teacher.

Working Stiff

The summer before my senior year, I worked
for the number-one Syracuse plumber
to save up for college room and board.

I joined four men, real working stiffs,
cracked skin over thick fingers and thumbs.
They called me Doc for my future career,
told me I'd chosen a long row to hoe.

To work with them, I had to fit in,
learn the skills of the plumbing trade:
jackhammer hard pavement, dig deep in long
ditches, lay sewer pipe down day in, day out,
in blazing hot sun or in soaking rain.

At the end of summer, Boss pulled me aside,
gave me a turn to ply the peak job of the trade: drive
his tanker truck through city streets, then empty
it into a drainage ditch not far from the city reservoir.

When I pulled myself up into the cab, I found
the rear window was cracked all across. Raw cesspool
sewage filled the tank just behind, easily seen
through a hole in the top. With a sudden jolt,
it could splash through the crack, onto my neck.

Slowly I drove through the streets of the city,
carefully using all gears, clutch, and brakes.
The fuel gauge, nearly empty, said I'd be foolish
to run out of gas with a load full of vile-smelling shit.

I eased the huge truck up the ramp of the first
gas station I saw, but could not stop its rocking motion
till I reached level ground. The station guy walked out,
held his nose, lifted a nozzle, pumped the gas.

When I extended my cash, he said with slight smile:
"Buddy, when you pull out, don't splash!"
I'd joined the ranks of working stiffs.

In the Footsteps of the Parisian Poet

Dutifully, he trails high heels clicking
up rickety stairs, treads so worn they could
have been climbed by Baudelaire on nightly
forays a hundred years before, howling
after one or more of his favorite whores.

The room is square, cracked ceiling, paint
peeling, washbasin at the wall, single bed
centered on the floor. His tutor, Piaf-like,
perhaps forty, orders him to drop his trousers
and drawers. With a flick of her tongue, he's
quickly undone. Wet washcloth tossed in the sink,
she remains standing, still fully clothed.

In his best college French he asks, *"Est-ce fini?"*
As she turns away, he exclaims, *"Vous m'avez trompé!"*
Mocking murmurs and laughter of other *putes*
de la rue Pigale rise through the window, cracked
open to the perfumed Parisian twilight.

That evening he hears a French couple
across the room undressing, caressing.
He listens to their rhythmic bedspring song,
stares at the ceiling above his hostel bed.

Forget-Me-Nots

While traveling abroad in his twenty-first year, he vowed to be true
to widening his views. He met a French girl who turned out to be true

to all he desired. For two weeks they discussed Voltaire and Camus
in a small Alpine village far up from view. This brief story is true.

She taught him to tie flowers both yellow and blue, into
garlands for her hair of *ne m'oubliez pas*, forget-me-nots, the true

translation. These days of dalliance wore on, became ever few,
till his vagabond life beckoned him once more to be true

to expanding horizons in strange lands and places, all new;
to heed Shakespeare: "This above all: to thine own self be true."

BECOMING AND BEING A DOCTOR

New York Central

We labored with crowbars, shovels, and picks,
digging deep ditches, replacing worn cables
along New York Central's railroad tracks,
my summer job between first and second
medical school years.

My mates were all working-class guys, who'd mostly
never made it through high school; their infrequent
words were loud and profane. When Friday payday
rolled around, one would shout out: "Man, today
that eagle gonna fly!" On the way home, they'd spend
much of their pay in a bar at the edge of town.

Four or five times each day a train passed us by,
its whistle a deep double shriek, its wheels a rising
crescendo of clickety-clacks. A distant light emerged
as an iron colossus, its engine sixteen feet high, cars
a mile or more long. If we caught his eye, the engineer
gave us a nod as his train roared by, scattering
waves of dust and debris on each side.

Back in school, I learned of histoplasmosis, a fungal
infection from Midwestern dust. My skin test
was positive, chest x-ray revealed typical specks—
a souvenir of my shifts by the railroad tracks.

I never saw my summer workmates again. After medical
school and training, my research focus was alcoholism.

Letter to Pa

I heard our tire chains clacking on slushy
streets, then waited freezing, short legs
dangling, watching you—warm coat
against the cold, your bag in hand—walk
through the opened door, return after
half an hour with a fresh loaf of bread, the way
you were paid in those late depression years.
A few years later, world war raging,
a neighbor's kid crossed the street
to beat me up. His dad was killed in France,
while you were safe behind the lines,
taking care of wounded men. I dreamed
each night of bombs and fires, invented
a secret rite to assure your safe return.
Ten years had passed when you divorced
my Ma and I had you for my own. I felt my
pride and your elation when you described
your research on zinc and B12.
I chose to follow your career, your footsteps,
as it's said, with twenty more years to train
till I became a medical scientist on my own.

When you died at seventy-eight, I was forty-
seven with thirty years more in my career.
My medical science and skills became
ingrained, within my deepest self. When
my career came to its end, I found myself
adrift, yet, always mindful, still your son.

I, Telemachus

A French general's wife in Casablanca
wrote in her last letter: "Forget me, all's over."
After my Pa came home from the War,
her hidden letters were found in a drawer.
Four years ago, we'd stood on the lawn
for a family portrait before he was gone.
I was just six, he uniformed, ready to cross
the ocean, care for sick soldiers.
After the move to LA when I was fourteen,
he divorced my Ma who returned to the East.
I had him to myself and thrilled to his tales
of caring for patients, research on malnutrition.
"I hope you weren't disappointed," he said, many
years later as we drove to his flight, "Of course not,
your talk was great," I replied. His medical career
was nearing its end. Mine was just beginning.

Grandma's Corpse

Each of sixteen shroud-covered corpses lay on a steel table, awaiting our first day of medical school. The windows opened to the street and the city graveyard beyond, marked with row upon row of granite headstones. When we pulled back the shroud, formaldehyde wafted up from someone's dead grandma or mum. We drew from four straws to decide who'd make the first cut. I picked up my scalpel and drew it through the skin of her bloodless chest and abdomen.

We each took a turn extending incisions, digging deep into the framework of her former life's functions. Her bloodless heart, a grapefruit, no longer pumped blood; her lungs, collapsed beach balls, no longer breathed air. We dissected each of twelve cranial nerves, conduits of life senses, their diverse roles learned by mnemonics bequeathed by students long gone. Lifting the veil of abdominal fat revealed her rubbery liver, an energy factory silenced by death, and her kidneys, toy footballs tucked up on each side. Her guts, former channels for food and waste, extended the length of the table she lay on.

Many weeks later, dissection done, all that remained were scraps of muscle and bone. Our corpse had made her final donation, the bedrock for each of our medical educations. Her remains had earned their rest in the cemetery across the street, after a spell in the hospital crematorium.

Tales out of Medical School

"On Old Olympus's Towering Top, a Fat-Assed German Viewed His Hops," and "Never Lower Tillie's Pants, Grand Mother Might Come Home," were mnemonics passed down from former anatomy students to remember the nerves in the head and bones in the wrist.

In first-year anatomy class, I shared a rectangular metal table with three other 21-year-old men and our assigned corpse, a blank-eyed, obese, and lifeless white seventyish woman. Half of my classmates were former Eastern prep school boys, the others mostly Jewish men from New York City. There were two women and two black men, one of them Ghanaian. I was the only one from west of the Mississippi.

Midway through, the Jewish guy next table over became unhinged, wondered if strips of skin from his assigned corpse could have been used to make Nazi lampshades at Auschwitz, only fifteen years before. He calmed down, later became a respected academic physician.

Two of the privileged former preppy guys thought it would be fun to terrorize our Ghanaian classmate. They came in the night and moved his assigned corpse to the floor. One crawled under the cover, groaned loudly when their classmate arrived. They achieved their aim, were never found out or expelled. The Ghanaian dropped out, went home at the end of the year.

During my third-year surgery rotation, I was lowest on the totem pole for surgical removal of a middle-aged woman's cancerous breast. I held the incision retractor for Doctor God, the surgeon in charge. Though God was highly respected within the city, the nurses knew He was actively drinking, clearly hung over, hands uncontrollably shaking. Halfway through, God's wobbling scalpel nicked open my retractor-holding thumb. Nothing was said by the resident doctors or nurses. I changed my surgical glove, carried on, and nothing else was ever done. For years, I worried that God had anointed me with transplanted breast cancer cells.

When I related this story at our 50-year reunion, two former preppies, each now a respected community physician, told our classmates that God was revered by his peers—there was no way this event could ever have happened.

Initiation Night

The pager beeps the end of my sleep. It's midnight; I'm the one on call. I quickly rise to make my way through basement tunnels where ancient pipes crisscross the ceilings, scuffs of gurneys mark the walls. Caged faint bulbs light the way, as they have for scores of interns for decades before.

I board the creaking lift to examine the newest patient, an alcoholic with liver failure in full DTs, then walk down the darkened hallway, enter each half-open door. Most of my patients sleep with their disorders; the eyes of the others reveal their fears. A homeless guy with frost-bitten feet seeks to survive the freezing northeastern winter. An aging hooker with acute PID has nowhere else to spend the night. A grizzled old man with pneumonia breathes fast, then shallow, coughs up putrid secretions that tell me his death is near. The remaining sick suffer other diseases, each one requiring my full attention.

The duty nurse, who's twice my age, asks which orders I'd like to change. I write down what seems best for each one's survival through the night. At six A.M., a glimmer of sun shines through the belching factory smoke of the city in its aging decay. As the nurse prepares to leave her station, her thanks say I'm now part of the healing profession.

Informed Consent

Outlined by the glimmer of eastern sun,
the head nurse tells me: "One of your
patients passed around four. His body's
been sent to the hospital morgue."

You're the intern, first up on the ward,
to see all the patients ahead of your team.
After four years of schooling, six months
on the job, you know what to do: preserve
life, prevent death, unless it's too late.

You must meet with his family, tell them
the news, get autopsy consent to learn why
he died. In this teaching hospital, sickness
and death are twin bases of your education.

When you sit down in private with three grown
orphaned children, you find they have no plan
what to do. His two daughters want him buried
intact. The oldest, his son, says, "So what
if he's gone?" His dad, a chronic alcoholic,
was always drunk, seldom home.

About this time, your chief resident calls, says
there's been a screw-up, the autopsy's been done.
He tells you to keep this news to yourself; you must
get the son to sign the post-hoc consent.

This after-death outcome's not in the Oath.
"Abstain from wrong-doing and harm" applies
to the sick, not the dead. Which is more harmful: telling
the truth, Dad's body's cut up and now gone, or stating
what's potentially true, so he'll sign the post-hoc consent form?

They argue, the daughters remorseful, the son angry,
unsure of his role. You decide on a time-worn approach
passed down from interns who came before.
You acknowledge their loss, then calmly advise:

"We think your Dad might have had TB. It could have
infected you all. Only an autopsy can tell." Your advice
permeates the room like stealthy fog. Finally, dead
silence is broken when the son stands up, says
"Fuck it," grabs the form from your hand, signs.

Bucket of Blood

He arrived at the ER half dead, stone drunk,
from the Bucket of Blood in Baltimore.
Feet frost-bitten, arms of a skeleton,
shaky hands, tongue red as a beet,
his eyeballs yellow as mustard.

Spider-web veins covered his chest;
gurgling noises rippled through his lungs.
Belly swollen, tender liver a basketball,
he babbled on with persons unknown.
Blood alcohol high, his outlook was grim.

Up on the ward, he puked up red blood.
Emergency scoping found a burst vein.
Blood pressure was low, pulse fast and weak,
but improved with transfusions of blood.
No one who knew him appeared.

Ten days later, he was ready to go:
no longer confused, blood tests improved,
eating well, as good as he would ever be.
His parting words: "Thanks, Doc, come
with me, I'll buy you a drink at the B of B."

Redemption

I'm high on crack and going eighty,
black rainy night, oncoming lights,
back seat guy shouts "Look out!" too late.
I cannot breathe, my chest's come tight.
Pain cuts my guts, knifes through to my back.
Ambulance screams, tears through the night.
ER docs crowd me, I'm under attack.
Up to the OR, all's black, nothing's right.
My guts are torn, they cut them out.
My fractured back will never be straight.
Condemned from now on to be fed by IV,
from gangbanger to cripple, that's now my fate.
My hospital room's filled with darkness, despair—
death's everywhere, in hallways, in air.
My past's come back, soon I must die,
when an angel as chaplain appears at my side.
She speaks of redemption and sin's retribution:
forgiveness of self is the final solution.
There's a way forward, of that I'm now certain.
I can pray to God, I need no permission.
I did not cheat death, I'm here for a reason.
My body's been broken, but my soul's been restored.
I'm reconnected to forces unseen,
I'm in spirit's realm, I've been redeemed.

Quality of Life

I slid in the scope past ridges and caves,
along a dark tunnel with purplish seams—
twisting and turning till finally it gave
out to a space where a pebbly lump gleamed.

From the end of the tunnel with purplish seams,
his life would be shortened by bloody ooze
into the space where the pebbly lump gleamed.
I slipped forceps through to give me a clue

from a piece of the lump with its bloody ooze,
which I sent to the lab to find out why he bled.
Cancer was the answer to the pebbly lump clue.
I'd have to tell him now, though the news would be dread.

When he awoke I told him why he bled.
"You've saved my life," was his reply.
Although the long-term prognosis was dread,
with surgery, he would not yet die.

To live life to the full was his reply
to the cards he'd been dealt by unwelcome fate.
Though his life might be short, he would not die
till he'd done all he could that remained on his plate.

For six long years he ignored his fate.
He traveled and painted, did all he had planned,
put aside all fears that remained on his plate,
till a spot appeared on a liver scan.

The cancer's return was not part of his plan.
Chemo became his only choice,
with puking and numbing and further scans,
until I had to tell him with quavering voice:

"No more can be done, you've no more choice,"
knowing full well that in weeks he'd be dead.
He rose from his chair and replied with clear voice:
"You gave me six years of life," was all that he said.

Tattoos

I consult on the ward for her malnutrition:
juvenile diabetic, now thirty-five,
paralyzed stomach, small intestine
partly removed. My prescription:
total nutrition at home by venous infusion.

She appears in clinic with a constant companion,
a woman her age always close by her side.
They find me culturally nonjudgmental,
responsive to all of her medical needs.

Amazing tattoos cover her arms, while
thumb-sucking Calvin stands guard by her scar.
A bright yellow sun radiates out
from her left upper arm, a goggle-eyed fish
swims by on the lower.

Hands behind head, mister M&M lounges
upon her right upper arm, gazes
down on two women's faces,
their lipsticked mouths barely touching.

My job: to assure her long-term survival,
through clinic visits, chart orders, long-distance
phone calls. They stay in touch when I retire,
send a trout-adorned mug for my birthday,
to recognize my dedicated medical care,
to make certain I know I remain in their lives.

Mouth to Mouth

Emerging from the swarming hornet horde,
I tear at seventy over the boundary bridge,
glance down at the dirty brown river, foresee
a straight shot through the traffic to home.

I scan the wetlands on either side.
A flock of crows hovers as one
above a marshland of brush and canals.
A great egret stands still, a white speck on a shore.

There's a cluster of cars on the shoulder.
Caution tells me it's time to slow down.
A big rig has pulled over. The driver
lies flat on his back on the ground.

My professional oath tells what I must do:
stop at the roadside, preserve life, prevent death.
I say the words that announce my profession.
The crowd retreats to the shoulder's outside edge.

I lean over to look at my patient, a fallen statue
in a sweat-soaked shirt, grossly obese with a slight drool.
I steel myself for mouth-to-mouth breathing, chest compressing,
releasing, to bring him back to inhale on his own.

I feel deep in his neck for a pulse, find none. His face is gray,
his eyes glazed. "Too late," I announce to the crowd,
"this man is already dead." A wailing ambulance crosses
the center divider, stops to load him aboard, and he's gone.

The egret flaps up from the marsh, circles overhead.
I return to my car, re-enter the freeway, slowly drive home.

Legacies

On a clinic visit she confided to me her ancestral African slavery, her people brought below decks in terrible chains to Trinidad to labor for generations for a succession of Spanish, British, French, and Dutch plantation owners. Freed in 1833 by British abolition, slaves continued to work as indentured servants, growing and harvesting the principal crop of sugar cane, which could be converted into coveted rum. In the next leg of triangular trade, rum was exported to the United States and back to Britain.

Coincidentally, in 1826 my fourth-generation forebear established the family fortune in a textile mill on the Merrimack in New England, where children were paid in pennies to make clothing out of cotton, the slave-dependent Southern crop decades before emancipation. Rum slaked the thirsts of the ruling class, the New England aristocracy, whose fortunes were made on the backs of these children and on the backs of African slaves and former slaves toiling in southern cotton fields and in cane fields under West Indian sun.

Navajo Medicine

Blustering winds foretold a desert storm,
spiraling sand a dark funnel cloud. Two teenage
boys climbed to the top of sacred Navajo
Mountain, silhouetted by darkening sky.

Lightning struck, sent a current through each boy
from head to toe. They arrived at our US Indian Hospital
in the back of a pickup truck: one stone dead,
the other babbling chaos.

We did what we could to keep him alive until *hatáli*,
the medicine man, appeared as if an apparition.
His diagnostic Hand Trembling rite revealed
imbalance of his patient's spirits.

The Holy People of Navajo Mountain
considered the climb a taboo transgression.
Exorcism of this grave offense required
the consummate Night Way incantation.

Hatáli sang and chanted nine days and nine nights
to restore the boy's ties with the Holy People,
to sustain tribal bonds while cleansing his soul,
to restore harmony to the Navajo Nation.

The Navajo boy walked away, while we *bilagáana*,
white doctors, stood silently by, awe stricken.

EXTENUATING CIRCUMSTANCES

Hopi Dancers

Since time out of mind, the Hopi tribe
maintained their customs, dances, beliefs,
then resisted conversions by Catholic priests.

Back in summer of '61, we, the only two whites,
stood quiet in the Oraibi *plaza* with reverent
native villagers, to witness ritual dances
of men and boys of the Hopi Nation.

For the warm-up dance to disparage the Spanish past,
two Hopi men dressed in black robes as priests of conversion.
Another played Christ with a crown of thorns, ascending
a ladder to Oraibi's roof of heaven. He was turned back
to the plaza by Hopi men at the top, who unzipped
and rained piss on the priests below.

In the rattlesnake pubertal rite, ten Hopi men,
each masked as a different animal spirit *kachina*,
encircled a closed wooden trunk. When the lid
was opened, each man reached in to grasp the neck
of a snake, sedated by darkness but ready to writhe.

Dancing in the circle to the sounds of thrumming drums,
each *kachina*-masked man passed his snake to a pubertal
boy, naked but for a loincloth. Each initiate placed the neck
of a snake in his teeth, continued the circular dance. After
ten turns, each snake was returned to the sandy middle.

Four well-chosen brave men dashed in, grabbed two
or three writhing snakes apiece by their necks, and raced
off to the desert in four compass directions. In this
fashion, each messenger snake from the holy ancients
was returned to its home in the Hopi Nation.

Feather River

While standing in California's Feather River
and casting my fly over rippling waters,
I remembered from passed-down family letters that
great-grandfather had mined for gold upstream.

Out from Boston, age twenty-five, he wrote
in letters home to his Ma: "The natives
in the woods nearby are not the noble savages
we've read about in Cooper's tales.

"Dirty blankets are all they wear,
with sticks in long and shaggy hair.
My friends go out to kill them for sport
on Sundays after noontime prayers."

Awaiting the pounce of an eager trout,
I recalled the widespread slaughter of native tribes
at the hands of miners and settlers
who lusted after their lives and lands.

When I came home with empty hands,
I opened a tiny box to gaze
on my inheritance, a golden wedding
band inscribed:

1855 one side,
Feather River on the other.

Whereas

Whereas, in 1637, my ancestor Samuel Appleton emigrated as a child from England to Massachusetts and later served as an officer in the colonial army, fighting against native tribes in King Philip's War,

Whereas, in 1855, my great-grandfather Greely Curtis came out from Boston to mine for California gold and witnessed Sunday afternoon killings of native peoples by miners along the Feather River,

Whereas, in 1855, his brother James Curtis was a San Francisco vigilante who shot natives for sport in San Mateo County,

Whereas, in 1961, I participated as a medical student in the care of sick Navajo people in Tuba City, Arizona and witnessed a Navajo medicine man save the life of a lightning-struck native boy,

Whereas, in 1973, I moved to Davis, California which was once populated by the Patwin Tribe, now extinct due to the 19th Century genocide of more than 80 percent of California natives,

Whereas, the sovereignty of native Americans is threatened by our present President, who has approved the Keystone Pipeline across Dakota territory and announced his intent to shrink native lands,

Therefore, as a United States citizen and three centuries descendant of a European immigrant, I declare that the rights of native Americans remain in jeopardy, perhaps now more than ever.

Black Lives

I'd read about beatings at lunch-counter sit-ins,
the shotgun slaying of Medgar Evers in Mississippi,
the Birmingham bombing, four Black girls killed,
Schwermer, Goodman, Chaney found dead in a levee.
It was nineteen sixty-four, not yet Blacks, but still Negroes,
their rights at the fore, each day more heady.
In medical training, I joined up in Cleveland, Ohio,
marched the streets with CORE and NAACP.
My main job was to sign up LBJ voters.
Someone said: "If LBJ loses, it's Blackbird bye-bye."
I volunteered to knock on doors in the ghetto,
an opportunity to change lives.
I walked unpaved streets, no sidewalks to be seen.
With their votes, black lives could be free.

Atrocities at Selma

Sit-ins, boycotts, freedom rides, marches
made civil rights a federal law
that promised equality for all races.
Yet racism prevailed in sixty-four;
voting rights for southern Blacks were still denied.
Tensions rose to a fever pitch
Blacks and whites came together in March sixty-five
to march across Selma's Pettus Bridge.
Police rioted, attacked marchers with gas and clubs.
A minister from Boston was later spied
in a downtown alley by local bat-wielding thugs.
The last words he heard before he died:
"Now you know what it's like to be
a nigger living and dying 'round here."

Voice from the Grave of Reverend Reeb

I was summoned to Selma in March sixty-five,
tearful Marie and four babies left behind.
I flew to that hellhole in Alabama to live out
my dream, to march for racial justice.

Dr. King had told us the way to freedom
is to conquer the fear of death. I prayed,
as he had taught, "for fearless courage to contend
against evil, to make no peace with oppression,
to strive for justice among all men and nations."

With Dr. King at the lead, we marched onto
the Pettus Bridge across the serpentine river
that wound through that hate-filled Southern state.

Exuberant Black and white ministers from
across the nation, we marched in solidarity,
each of us mindful we could together bend
the arc of racial justice toward equality.

Though stopped by all-white police mid-bridge,
we knew in our hearts that our march
for equal rights for all races must soon
become the law of the land.

Walking down a dark street after dinner
with two other Unitarian ministers, I heard
the shouts: "Hey, nigger-lovers!" Four men
crossed the street, raised weapons in hand.

With a face of pure hate, the one in the lead
swung his bat full force on my skull, crushed
my life which I gave for equal rights.

My 1967 War

Nine months before the Arab-Israeli six-day war of 1967, I joined the US Naval Medical Research Unit in Cairo and moved to a suburb with my wife and infant son. American phones were tapped; Egyptian colleagues never came to our homes, presuming any of us could be CIA spies for Israel, just a day's drive away. When Egypt took over the Suez Canal in May, American wives and children were ordered to leave. My colleagues and I caravanned to work.

On June fifth, I spotted a solitary plane, a speck in the sky above our workstation. In the Israelis' first foray, they destroyed the Egyptian air force on the ground, just thirty miles away from us. Our anxiety grew when Radio Cairo reported the Israeli Army's advance across the Sinai desert. On June ninth, the day before the war ended, the Egyptian army blew up their munitions, lest they fall into enemy hands.

At midnight, the American embassy called: now was the time to leave. We boarded a train at Cairo station bound for Alexandria, where a Greek cruise ship would take us to safe haven in Athens. As the train pulled away, lines of peasants stood by the tracks, shaking their shoes, soles facing us, the ultimate sign of Arab contempt.

We awaited the cruise ship in Alexandria's port, hoping it would be large enough to transport us to Athens. Chugging under a star-filled canopy, we never knew of the Israeli air attack two days before that killed thirty-four American sailors on the nearby US reconnaissance ship Liberty—the attack was not in the script, only reported by the American press years later.

After five months of dalliance with my family in Greece, I was among the first Americans to return to Cairo. On my first evening back, four Egyptian policemen banged on my door to report how they had guarded our home, prevented attacks by marauding defeated Egyptians. I knew it was baksheesh they wanted, and I rewarded them handsomely.

Our cook arrived from across the Nile. He told me he'd care for my needs, said it was wrong to live alone. He offered a temporary village wife. I politely refused.

Belly Dances

The first American doctor returning to Egypt after the '67 war,
I was bitten by a rabid dog near the Great Pyramids. More than
two feet high, it tore in growling from the desert, plunged its teeth
deep into my thigh. I knew without treatment I could die.

I rushed to my office at our research station in Cairo,
found a key, unlocked a drawer, found the precious
anti-rabies serum. Each day for fourteen, I filled a syringe,
swabbed my belly with alcohol, plunged the needle in.
*

A fiftyish American man stopped by our sick bay, on the way
for a heart transplant in Capetown. His heart was enlarged
with a rapid beat. Both lungs displayed scattered gurgling,
signs of serious illness. He was too sick to treat here.

We took the next flight out to Beirut, a ninety-minute trip.
A tire-screeching ambulance ride through ancient twisting
potholed streets brought us to the American Hospital ER,
where I dropped him off, saw him no more.
*

Awaiting the next plane home, I read in the English language
newspaper that the belly dancer Atouta, *aka* Little Cat, was
playing at the Kit Kat Klub. I'd seen her in Cairo before the war,
dancing for Jean-Paul Sartre and Simone de Beauvoir.

After I seated myself near the stage, Atouta appeared with silken
scarf around her neck, undulating belly bare, coins jangling from
her hips and brassiere. To the sounds of tambourine, drum, oud,
and finger cymbal tak-a-taks, she performed her mesmerizing dance.

Extenuating Circumstances

Sacramento, California, *2013*
Car runs over black man
in downtown shopping mall.
Driver tells police he deserved it.
"Now that they have Obama,
they think they're just real special."

Phoenix, Arizona, *2012*
Two hundred Mexican-Americans
arrested, jailed in tents at 120 degrees.
Sheriff Joe tells the press:
"So it's O.K. for our soldiers to live in hot tents,
but it's wrong for inmates here?"

Haditha, Iraq, *2005*
Children shot in pajamas, father with his Koran,
twenty-four in one family gunned down.
Blood-spattered beds, furniture, walls,
"To teach them a lesson they'll never forget:
all terrorists must die."

My Lai, Vietnam, *1968*
Babies bayoneted, mothers machine-gunned,
terrified children cower behind.
Huts burned down by Zippos to the thatch,
three hundred and more. *"They must be VC.*
All commies must be killed."

Selma, Alabama, *1965*
Northern white Unitarian minister
joins civil rights march at Pettus Bridge,
dies after blow to head with baseball bat.
Last words he hears: *"Now you know*
what it's like to be a nigger around here."

Bullard's Bar, California, *1855*
My great-grandfather digs for gold,
writes home to his mother in Boston:
"The Indians here are not the noble
savages of Fenimore Cooper; my friends
shoot them on Sunday afternoons."

Homeless Shelter

The nomadic poor of our town trudge silently through
the gate, check in at our program site for an overnight stay
at one of the churches nearby. The men wear five-day
stubbles, women threadbare sweaters, old clothes.
A volunteer, I serve coffee, observe, provide a listening ear.

An old man with a grease-spattered shirt and wobbly
gait appears burnt out from years of sloshing down booze.
An aged woman in unwashed clothes grasps
at my sleeve, mutters her woes. A well-dressed young
woman in a red beret stares quietly down at the floor.
A shitfaced young guy with slurred speech starts a fight;
we call the town cops who take him away.

A tall black guy with an afro stands still as a statue,
meditating against an inside wall. An ex-con
with skull and snake tattoos needs a bus pass to meet
his parole. Two outcast young lovers, hands together,
long for better days. A businessman tells us his wife
kicked him out, silently scans the *New York Times*
to show us he's not of their kind.

Tomorrow, some will seek work and a place to live, but most
will shuffle the streets until dark, wait for spring's return
to reclaim their old spots by the tracks out of town.

Driving the Homeless

After winter check-in, I drive them
to overnight shelter, a different church
each week in our town. A retired physician,
it's my chance to rekindle compassion.

Monday
The brown-faced young woman beside me
clutches her knapsack, stares at the floor,
declines to respond when I ask where she's from.
A loud young guy in the backseat boasts
of the .44 pistol he once owned, the five years
he served down south in state prison.

Tuesday
A college grad I knew from last year
grabs the seat beside me, starts a recitation
to make sure the others know he's down
on his luck for now, just a brief dislocation.

Wednesday
A middle-aged woman trashes my views
when I flip off the radio news of our leader
whose favorite cause is immigrant bashing.
A tall black guy sits still in the backseat
while a skinhead in a Raiders T-shirt squeezes
his bulging muscles into the opposite corner.

Thursday
A loud-mouthed young guy in the backseat, slurred
speech like he's been drinking, starts to jostle
the woman beside him. I pull to the side of the road,
take his pack from the trunk, tell him it's time to go.

Friday
Bill, wearing a watch cap and stubble beard, whom I'd met
a couple of years ago, tells me that Richard—the man
I'd pulled out of a drainage ditch last year—died
last week while lighting up stoned in his sleeping bag.

The Handout

Driving into the shopping center, I see a woman hold up a sign: HELP ME, MY HUSBAND JUST DIED! About fifty, brown face and scraggly black hair, she wears a man's threadbare coat, holds out a cap for some change. Avoiding eye contact, exiting drivers turn the corner, speed away. Is this just a scam or a chance to do good? Would my gift be used for drugs, booze, or food? When I'm ready to leave, should I avert my eyes or come to a stop at her side? I check my wallet: a few twenties, none smaller. When I hold out a twenty, she draws my hand to her mouth, plants a wet kiss. Tears streaming, she murmurs, "Muchas gracias, señor."

stopped at a side street
sunset gleams off rearview mirror
I wipe off my hand

Victims Remain in Our Prayers

"He was disturbed," the Tehama neighbors said,
often awakened at dawn by automatic rifle blasts.
The night before, he shot his spouse dead, hid
her body under floorboards. On rampage morning,

he killed five neighbors, wounded seven kids locked
for safety at their school, was finally shot by the cops.
The townspeople knew he was evil. One said:
"He should never been able to own firearms."

This was nothing compared to Texas First Baptist,
twenty-six dead in November, and of course
there's Vegas in October, the record so far,
fifty-nine killed by a gunman acting alone.

The day after Vegas, our esteemed Senate leader
declared, "It's just too soon for discussion,
the victims remain in our prayers." So far,
nothing about Tehama, just another mass murder.

My Civil War Sword

Willed to me by my mother, my Civil War
sword hangs from two closet hooks screwed
into my office wall. My great-grandfather
used it in battle one hundred fifty-five years ago.

The sword is three feet long, gently
curved. Its brass filigreed grip is protected
by a fenestrated guard that boldly displays
US, the Union side.

Great-grandfather's name adorns the top
of the scabbard. A Massachusetts Cavalry
colonel, enlisted at thirty two, he battled
Confederate rebels over three long years.

When the sword is pulled from its scabbard
and extended full length, *E Pluribus Unum*
is etched across the blade. The edge
is dulled, but the point remains sharp.

Dark brown streaks tarnish the bottom
third, perhaps dried rebel blood
from the great-great-grandpa of one
of Charlottesville's hooded Klansmen.

The Minotaur Never Sleeps

A fog of fear descends upon the land.
The Minotaur who never sleeps has left
the depths of his labyrinth.

His grip of power complete,
his early morning tweets threaten
the sanctity of our lives, demolish our hopes.

His brutal commands: to banish throngs
of brown-skinned immigrants behind a wall
of hatred the length of our southern border,

to shred longstanding alliances,
to foment religious fears, to forge
new links with tyrants abroad.

Will the beast be overcome before he
triggers the nuclear codes? Will our Theseus
come before this monster's work is done?

Torn Fabric

I.

The homeless of our town trudge through the gate
of our intake center, jostle in line to avoid a night
in freezing rain. Tomorrow, they'll shuffle the streets
until dark, wait for spring to reclaim dry ground
near the ditch by the railroad tracks.

II.

I've heard it told the half-man, half-beast is loose
upon the land. He brooks no dissent, cares little
or nothing for homeless poor, banishes strangers
from our midst, rips through the tapestry of our lives.

III.

At misty dawn at the pond, I watch an orange-billed
cormorant fatefully flap its black wings, ascend
to a pinpoint in the sky. Mid-morn at the market, I learn
the falafel and baba ghanoush stall is gone. Last night,
glass windows and doors of our town's Islamic Center
were smashed, bacon strips wrapped around doorknobs.

IV.

The rough beast whose time is come has slouched
his way to Washington. Its presidential tweets inform
@realPOTUS: THE AMERICAN DREAM IS BACK!

Moon Over the High Rise

Our President, returned triumphant from shaking hands
with "so-called leaders" of foreign lands, tweets
"Success for all Americans!" There's "no decision
yet on Paris Accord"—sustain it to help the solar guys
or shred it to please his pals in oil and coal.

All bets say he'll stick with oil and coal. He thinks
putting down those foreign losers would be just what
they deserve. Meanwhile, the moon does its thing—
it's not just an orb that floats in the sky—it pulls
out the tide, pulls it back in.

Warmer water melts Arctic ice, makes oceans rise, slosh
over beaches onto avenues, let's say in New York on Fifth,
where our gold-plated leader visits his penthouse.
He shoves his ample arse out his top-floor window,
moons us mere citizens swimming above the sidewalks.

Christmas Mass

A life-sized wooden cross hangs over the altar:
dying Jesus suspended from spiked ankles and wrists.
Streaks of blood ooze from his spear-ripped liver.

The pious walk down the aisle, genuflect, move on.
We sit quietly by, share the guilt of the cross.
The only innocents are just-baptized infants.

A procession of golden frocks moves slowly down the aisle,
open jars of incense swing back and forth, left then right.
Choking on wooden benches, we await the main event.

The head priest delivers a lengthy parable of powers:
who is the strongest, Superman or Jesus?
Shifting in our seats, we already know.

At last, the mysterious eucharist. The parishioners line up
to receive chunks of bread, sip wine from a silver chalice—
the transubstantiated flesh and blood of crucified Jesus.

A junior priest appears, gathers up the bread,
swigs down the remaining blood of Jesus
mixed with the spittle of sinning parishioners.

Saturday Farmers' Market

Here's how it goes at our Farmers' Market:
shoppers all ages, clothing, and races;
parents push bundled babies in strollers,
children dash eagerly through the crowd.
Others meander to and fro, seeking
new food and old faces they know.
At the top are the hucksters and politicians
handing out stickers, buttons, petitions.
There's music: guitars, banjos, accordions,
fiddlers, and a guy playing a digeridoo.
There's lines for coffee, authentic Peruvian,
for fresh-baked bread: ciabatta, focaccia;
for pasta: fettucine, tagliatelle, agnolotti, maccheroni,
chitarra; for cheese: Locarno, cheddar, gouda, and brie.
There's heirloom tomatoes, bok choy, lettuce, kale,
Swiss chard, Satsuma mandarins, Fuyu persimmons,
just-ripened peaches, nectarines, pears,
fresh strawberries, blueberries, plums,
just-caught mackerel, salmon, sole, and

a homeless guy peddling his *Sparechanger* rag.

There's just-caught mackerel, salmon, sole,
fresh strawberries, blueberries, plums,
just-ripened peaches, nectarines, pears,
Swiss chard, Satsuma mandarins, Fuyu persimmons.
There's heirloom tomatoes, bok choy, lettuce, kale;
cheese: locarno, cheddar, gouda, brie;
pasta: fettucine, tagliatelle, agnolotti, maccheroni, chitarra;
and fresh-baked bread: ciabatta, focaccia.
There's lines for coffee, authentic Peruvian,
and music: fiddlers, a guy playing a digeridoo,
guitar, banjo, and accordion players.
At the top, handing out stickers, buttons,
petitions are hucksters and politicians.
Seeking new food and old faces they know,
are others meandering to and fro.

Children dash eagerly through the crowd, their
parents push bundled babies in strollers.
With shoppers all ages, clothing, and races,
that's how it goes at our Farmers' Market.

RAINBOW RIDE

Magpies in Ascendance

There's a sequence of birdsongs at dawn:
the distant moan of the mourning dove,
chirping crescendos of sparrows,
shrill wrenks of scrub jays,
loud caw-caws of crows,
the kut-kuts of the magpies, like wood
sliding down a washboard.

Opening the door to our deck I'm greeted
by a cautious squirrel peering down
from a tree branch. A sudden flurry
of blue wings, flashing white breasts—
two kut-kutting magpies bear down
to flap the intruder off to our neighbor's rooftop.
Now they're back in the treetops, declaring
rule over their territory, our backyard.

They strut brazen near the edge of the road,
not three feet from passing cars, picking over
sticks and nuts dropped from trees by crows.
They don't care if I stop to admire their bright
yellow bills, white breasts, blue bodies, long tails,
or if I walk right up and look them straight
in the eye, to ask why they've flown in
to spend this season with us.

Is it to remind us they've lived here
for two million years, many times longer
than our foolish species has walked the earth,
carving it up and spewing pollution
into the over-heated atmosphere? Is it to tell
us we're the true interlopers on their stage?

For after we've melted the polar icebergs
and the coastal rivers have risen to flood
our valley, the magpies will just move
up to the foothills. God's flying creatures
will evolve and survive long after we're gone.

Return of the Magpies

Two each to a silvery leaf-bare branch,
eight sit still in our front yard birch,
heralding the season's change,
sharp yellow bills, white breasts,
wings and tails of green and blue.

Overhead more call out kut-scree,
declaring their space from caw-cawing
crows in hasty retreat far from our
neighborhood trees. How did they know
they'd find safe haven here?

Why such precision of colors to bring
enchantment to my day? Is it all in their DNA?
O master molecule of life! Your helical staircases
uncoiled, an arm's length in each cell,
each helix linking quaternary codes

in sixty-four permutations,
unzipping and doubling as cells divide,
transcribing the codes
for the proteins that signal
all intricate processes of life,

that make yellow bills, white breasts,
dark blue wings, long tails to fly,
all the flight maps in their brains,
their kut-kut scree-scree songs,
their monogamous matings to survive,

while my own DNA creates vision,
finds beauty in this first sign of spring,
as the same quaternary codes
spin spiral staircases in my brain,
transcribe the signals that discover
mystery in DNA, miracles in magpies.

Rainbow Ride

We rode out on a late winter morning,
a fast trot atop a levee by a farm ditch in our valley
that stretches from Shasta to Tehachapi,
from the Sierra Nevada to the western hills,
now greenish gray and ever in our distance.

We tripped along the roadway splashing mud on either side,
his nostrils flared, ears upright with fine-tuned hairs,
wind-tossed mane, his pounding muscles next to mine,
as I, close reined, captured his power with my legs,
crotch, and spine, and the earth called out to us.

We thought we'd find old friends who'd tell
of the coming spring: the great heron in the reeds
of a close-by pond where fish are seen jumping
on warmer days, the red-winged blackbirds
that sit on the phone lines and sing to the wind.

Jackrabbits zigzagged up and down the plain,
just-flushed quails tore across our view,
chirping sparrows wheeled about, and the great heron
rose up, wings flapping, and settled in a distant field.

Dark clouds came down to wash our faces
with Pacific rain, then gave way as sun-washed
green grass foretold the season's change.

Pacific Daybreak

Dawn rims the mountains across the bay.
Waves roll and crash in eternal show;
bursting foam heralds the newborn day.

Glints on the sea reflect sun's rays.
Waves reach skyward as sea winds blow;
dawn rims mountains across the bay.

Searching shorebirds skip along the quay.
Waves break like shots on rocks below;
bursting foam heralds the newborn day.

Brightening sun is filtered by spray.
Sea rushes up in ebb and flow;
dawn rims the mountains across the bay.

Pungent odors pervade the air.
Waves recede when tide is low;
seaweed is unveiled by light of day.

Underground creatures are thrown in the fray;
life spawns on rocks beneath the foam.
Dawn rims mountains across the bay;
bursting foam heralds the newborn day.

Fault-Line Fury

The laboratory rocks like a boat
on a choppy sea. Swaying, wobbling,
I grasp at the counter's edge. Underground
demons thrust me forward, back.

Terrified, I imagine walls
toppling, ceiling collapsing.
Half-full flasks fall sideways,
sulfurous gases fill the air,

broken glassware covers
the floor. Outside roof ledge
cracks, crashes onto courtyard. Shaking
stops. It's 5:04. Fifteen seconds: gone.

Commuters pack the station. Trains are still, awaiting
word of damaged track. Phone lines downed, I contemplate
my terrified wife alone in our swaying top-floor apartment.
Aftershocks rumble, perhaps preamble to apocalypse.

At twilight I squeeze into the last remaining bus.
It lumbers chockful down the highway past caved-in
rooftops. Great steel birds choke runways, others
circle aimlessly overhead, no place to land.

The wounded city awaits our return. Power is out, brick walls
collapsed. Fires light the northern horizon. Trembling
and alone, I step off the bus into darkness for my long walk home
past extinguished streetlights and quavering walls.

The Bird Beyond My Window

I wrack my brain for something new to write,
try combinations of former poems, but mine
must be original, self-plagiarism not allowed.
I glance out my window, gaze over my lawn.

There it is! On top of a post about three feet high,
(I drove it into the ground last spring), there's
a medium-size bird with a black head and neck.
I raise my binocs, train them outside for a look.

It's maybe eight inches long, gray body, wings,
and tail, white belly, sharp beak. I grab
my bird book, take another look, but it's gone.
Could be a black phoebe, cannot be certain.

But I know all its movements are driven
by species-specific bird DNA, the master
molecule for all forms of life, that makes it
sit still, glance toward me in fright,
push off to find safety in the nearest tree.

Winter Landscapes

As I gaze westward from my sixth-floor perch,
green fields and tree rows stretch for miles.
An orange sunset glints distant rays
through the faraway coast range saddle,
carved out by the creek where swim
the descendants of ancient trout.

Flocks of caw-cawing crows sail past my window,
rush to distant trees before nightfall.
With subtle cut-cuts the magpies,
white breasts, gold beaks, blue tails,
gather in a nearby tall tree to hold their ground.

A flap of great wings: the magpies are gone
when a red-tailed hawk settles at tree top.
With crooked beak and beady eyes,
it searches for creatures far below,
perhaps a foolish field mouse
venturing out to the fading light.

The hawk gives up, glides off.
Magpies return, darkness falls.

Elegant Jewels

A well-dressed woman with elegant jewels
sits at the lobby window looking like
a high-end hooker awaiting her mark
and his unlimited expense account.

Outside, cars move two abreast, timing
traffic lights between walls of expensive
boutiques, glittering restaurants, art
galleries awaiting tourist discovery.

Homeless teenagers seeking handouts stand
among passed-out drunks on the sidewalks,
while church crosses mark distant
neighborhoods of well-kept houses and lawns.

From the window of my ninth-floor room,
I gaze toward distant forested mountains.
A snow-capped volcano rises sharply
above the horizon, while the narrow arc

of a gleaming river promises hungry fish
migrating to their birthplaces far from sea,
challenges me to connect my line and hook
with millennia of evolution.

A swooping flock of tree swallows abruptly
threatens collision, then at the last second
veers away from my window, flashing
white breasts in the late morning sun.

In the Canyon

Oh! To catch a fish—a fine slippery trout!
To feel a jerk, a sudden connection
with primordial creature, to pull him out

from flowing current would be total perfection,
an answer to years of seeking
life's greater meaning, a new dedication

to keep open my mind with no weakening
of resolve to find miracles each day
in the beauty of my surroundings.

There was a cold winter mist as I made my way
on a path through a canyon of eons of stone,
past grasses and bushes brown and wintry gray.

High above wheeled hawks, eyes piercing the gloom.
Below me, the river held creatures of ages,
ancient insects and fishes, as I, all alone

gazed downward, heart pounding in stages
of anticipation, my goal now at hand,
heightened by splashes and circles of waves,

certain signs that fish were out there to land,
while my skills from years of this sport
of casting and hooking were at my command.

Excitement grew as I made way to the shore
through moss-covered rocks and tangles of vines.
I stepped into calm eddy and current before

me, when a call from across river and far above land
engaged my attention: high gliding wings
revealed an osprey seeking prey, nature's plan.

Below, brown speckled trout, eight or nine,
darted to and fro, up river and down,
while tiny white flies beclouded the air, sure sign

that my fake fly, if perfectly thrown
from the end of the line cast across and upstream,
would float down the current and soon be devoured

by a bug-mistaken fish that hooked would be seen
jumping in air, then, in watery rout
till exhaustion, brought up to my creel.

Yet many fine casts, each made as if new,
to each innocent fish went unheeded,
though visible fins and loud splashes made sure I knew

they were all in the current. Yet, food was not needed,
for in this moment, something else was at hand:
a natural prayer that new life would be seeded.

I peered through watery film to find
a roiling mound of fish. Two trout faced upstream,
the female held still, eggs trailing behind,

while the dominant male released
a cloudburst of sperm, for his ultimate deed
was to fertilize eggs while promoting creation.

A shriek broke the air and, for all nature to see,
from downriver the osprey tore through the mist,
wings flapping wide, a trout clutched in its claws.

Standing in the Stream

White water torrents over upstream rocks;
fast-roiling currents gradually calm
to gentler riffles where I can stand.

It arises from far wet mountainside patches
pushed upward by relentless grinding of tectonic
plates, earth's crust moving in from the sea.

Through countless millennia, the stream
carves its niche through canyons of rock,
spawns multitudes of living creatures,

then drops thousands of feet to valley
woodlands and marshes, enters the river
that flows to the sea.

I hear birdsong from tangled vines
along the shore, smell fragrant blossoms,
feel warm springtime on my face,

the freshness of onrushing water.
I await with full intention the sudden
dart of the trout.

When it grabs my hook,
it connects through the line to my soul.
Millennia become my present.

To Catch a Steelhead at Dawn

You must set your alarm at half past four.
To meet your guide, drive forty miles or more.
It's dark as pitch at boat launch on the river.
The hull rocks as you board, your heart's aquiver.

The dawn's just a sliver of sun in the east.
The early light of October foretells later feast.
The roiling river surface reveals thrashing tails
as salmon shower sperm on the eggs of their females.

But the prey that you seek lies downstream of the spawn.
The steelhead trout dance for the eggs starts right at dawn.
You must outwit your great fish by your cast of fake fly
to fall just upstream of where the fish lies.

Its grab sends a jolt up your line—you must
jerk your rod straight back to set your hook.
Your fish will then turn to race down the stream;
to shake itself loose, it will jump and careen.

If you keep just the right tension hard on your reel,
excitement will build with each fish move you feel.
When at last your steelhead trout starts to tire,
you must wind your reel fast if you aspire

to bring it up to your net and to land by the range
of orange-flamed trees that announce season's change.

Song of the Steelhead Trout

My stuttering line came tight at early dawn,
sure sign I'd hooked a large steelhead trout
in fast roiling water, the spawning ground.

I jerked back my rod, set hook in fish mouth,
lowered the rod-tip, loosened the line as it leapt
and careened its way downstream in frantic rout.

With line held tight, I reeled the huge fish to my net,
carefully walked it to shore, the sun now fully out.
Three feet in length, its belly and sides were flecked

with white sperm. I had hooked a female steelhead trout
in the very act of sex. I lifted it carefully from the net, put
it down upon the ground, turned to find a large stone

to bash in its head, then slice it open to yank out its guts.
When I turned back to gaze with pride on my prize,
I found a coquette standing before me with rosebud

nipples and flowing black hair. My hand on her spine,
I felt with surprise a slimy green bottom and tail.
I lowered her gently back in the stream and gazed

sadly away as she left me alone with nary a trail.
Released from my embrace, my river princess
swam back to rejoin the ongoing orgy of spawn.

Upside Down

Inferno

Upside down in fast-moving current, my death but seconds away:
boulders below, the demons who'd break my bones,
branches above, the harpies who'd end my day.

Eyes fixed on a bank-side bloom, I'd pulled the wrong oar,
while fishing the great Rogue River alone.
My pontoon boat had flipped when it met the shore.

From deep within came a voice without sound
that broke through my terror, as if in a dream:
"If I can keep my head on straight, I will not drown."

I jerked the cord to inflate my vest when I was far downstream.
Breaking surface upright, survival became my only aim.
I gained a foothold, breathed deeply in, surveyed the scene.

Purgatorio

Waves crashing on rocks below meant certain death by maiming,
but the river above flowed smooth as glass as my very own
capsized boat and one oar floated down. My life could be sustained.

I swallowed my pride to have fished the river alone,
recanted all the audacity left in my soul,
grasped the oar and boarded my boat, though it was upside down.

Stroking hard to escape the demon rocks, I paddled my pontoon
across the river with strength I'd never known
and reached a place where I could turn it upright, a quiet lagoon.

Paradiso

I spied two fishermen in their boat about fifty yards below.
They rowed to me with a second oar, a rescue from my plight,
since the journey downstream to takeout was still a mile-long row.

I drifted slowly, songbirds singing, watching ducks alight.
A treetop eagle spied a fish that soon would pay its cost.
Deer bowed their heads to drink; geese soared above in flight.

Making landfall at last, I was met by a fisherman host.
With outstretched hand, one said: "Here, take this cold beer!"
I'd reached a grace I vowed would never again be lost.

SENIOR MOMENTS

Waking Rituals

At first light, the cars below begin to move.
I hear the distant moan of the early dawn freight;
closer in, the gentle coos of the mourning dove.

Still in cocoon, I roll towards
her sleep-shrouded nakedness,
spoon my bony angles around soft curves.

I'm awake and alive, while with
rhythmic rise and fall of her rib cage
she sleeps on warm and still.

Birds start to call, some shrill, some peeps.
Low washboard stutters of magpies
announce the gathering light of the sun.

Gray turns to gold across fields of wheat,
distant oaks from dark to brilliant greens.
Sunlight bursts through close-in leaves.

I splash cold water on my face,
get the tea water up to a boil.
Scalding heat, oxygen, tiny leaves

burst magical aromas and tastes
all the way from Ceylon to my brain.
My senses now at their height,

I move into my day.

The Watch Fixer

Thunderstorms ahead. Fuel low.
We must divert the plane.

The cross-country flight veers sharply north.
In the event of a water landing. . .
Heart pills in pocket, pulse steady,
leave all personal items behind.

I look down. My watch has stopped.
A solid black face, its silver hands gauge time.
Smaller rings mark weekday and date.
One loose ring traps the minute hand.

My watch has stopped.
From the faraway airport,
I drive alone in a rented car
on untraveled two-lane roads,

through thunderclaps, lightning crackles,
strange landscapes in the darkening mist.
I arrive at the old family house on the shore
where my mother was born.

She's now buried in the garden below
the rain-spattered windows of my childhood.
My watch has stopped.
Sun breaks through the dawn.

In town the expert watch fixer
lifts off the crystal, frees the minute hand.
Handing back the watch, she smiles.
The second hand sweeps on:

a lifetime of minutes, hours, days.

Mockery

How to create something from nothing,
meaning from meaningless? Relentless
time ticks on, minute by minute. The wall
to ceiling bookshelves across the room

mock me with millions of meaningful words.
Inspiration eludes; I'm in desperation mode.
The cracked-open window lets in a breeze;
its soft wind blows through to my ear.

A high-pitched chirping sequence of tunes:
the mockingbird calls from a distant tree.
The old couple across the street hunch
over their garden, oblivious to sound,

while the distant high-pitched recital
stirs synapses in my brain. Far down
the street from my second-floor perch,
black crows patrol the neighborhood.

One screeches control from the highest tree.
Magpies alight nearby with fluttering wings.
Their gold beaks, white bodies, black tails,
low washboard sounds call out just to me.

My brain's now awake and I pick up my pen.

I Wake Up Weary and Realize I'm Really Getting Old

Did I really drive from Escalante to the Navajo Reservation (now Nation) over a lunar landscape? Did the highway lose its landmarks? Was my '91 maroon Beamer really marooned atop a massive rock not far from Four Corners, crevasse on either side, crescent canyon barely seen below? Did I creep along the rock-strewn road, at my wild wits end, to reach a zigzag dirt road dropping down at least a mile to the winding river below? Did an arrogant tourist in an oversized RV with Jersey plates rip past me, middle finger raised, on the inside of a curve? Am I really now wide awake at 5 AM, safe, sound, and alive in my bed, beside my faithful wife of thirty years?

The Odyssey of Retirement

Odysseus, the bastard son of Sisyphus,
sailed by the stars of his destiny,
outlasted the ire of Poseidon,
who sent searing sun,

gales and freezing rains
to punish his audacity
for blinding the one-eyed Cyclops,
sailing past the Sirens' songs of desire,

seducing the goddess Circe, and
feasting on the cattle of the gods.
A seer from hell foretold his choice,
just one of two paths to be taken

as his hair turned gray,
his skin more weathered:
to plant his oar in Ithaca,
renounce the sea,

till the soil and savor his wine,
lie down again with Penelope,
or to presume his youth once more,
set sail to taunt the gods of destiny

and die by wreckage on a rocky shore,
never to find the paradise of heroes
at the far edge of the western stars.

Shimmering Stream

An old geezer patrols the sidewalk near my political sign, wears a Raiders cap and a leather jacket with cracks on its sleeves, like it's been run over too many times. Through a hole in his scraggly beard, he clenches a cigar butt in his teeth, spits black tobacco juice onto the ground, holds tight to a lurching bulldog's leash. I've seen them once before, same place, same time, when he answered my greeting with a grunt that said fuck off, don't mess with us. This time, he glances toward the sign, bristling like a pissed-off porcupine.

The bulldog strains at the leash, then stops at the edge of my yard and my newly planted grapefruit tree. When the geezer relaxes his grip, the bulldog lifts its closest back leg, lets loose a shimmering stream of piss like a blast from the nozzle of a garden hose. It splashes like fizzy champagne on my sign and drops onto my ground-cover bark.

Once they're out of sight, I walk out to my tree, see drops on its leaves, while the sign still shimmers with pee. I walk back inside with a simmering brain, pick up my pen, another pissed-off porcupine.

Five Haiku

hummingbird hovers
bare trees fallen leaves
black cat sets to pounce

crows cover the sky
sweep in from fall horizon
shit on parking lots

red toyon berries
autumn jewels adorning hedge
neighbor's chainsaw growls

dark shapes thrashing tails
autumn salmon spawn
their bodies line the shore

autumn sunsets
golden fields
beware! cracked pavement

My Case of Shingles

A black cat has leapt without warning,
claws fully drawn, ready to rip
the skin off my back, render it
angry, red, and swollen.

The feline demon draws its
claws across my naked flesh.
I'm bare and helpless on the sheet.
Each open sore turns into ooze.

Its ceaseless claws dig deeply into
the core of my hopeless mind.
A helpless bird within its grasp,
I'm slowly being tortured to death.

A centipede scurries left to right
across my raw and bleeding back.
Tiny feet tease open every scab
that seeks in vain to form.

A carrion crow lands on my back,
pecks sharply into every welt. It's
found a half-dead rabbit, jerks
out its entrails piece by piece.

They draw blood from my hide,
suck out my soul,
squeeze joy from my day.
Why don't they just turn

their attacks on another prey,
just leave me alone
to revel in the cool
autumn breeze?

Twelve-Step Dante

Two thirds through my life's journey,
I found myself lost in a dark tangled wood.
The way to the light was obscure to me.

As if in a dream, I wandered about,
my demons confusion and fear.
My mind was in turmoil, clouded with doubt.

One by one, three fearsome beasts appeared:
a leopard of sloth, greed, and desire,
a lion of pride, my frightful barrier

against all who'd support me through the mire,
a wolf raging at fate with darkness all around.
Anxiety grew. I could not aspire

to comfort, when a voice within me spoke without sound:
"If I will accept what cannot be revised,
each day will have meaning, spirit my ground."

Within me dwells my spirit of life,
my constant guide to all that's kind.
Aware of life's mystery, beauty, and gifts,

I can receive when I open my mind
to everyday miracles that transform the night.
If I seek and listen, soon I will find

a life free from fear, with faith and insight,
acceptance, the serenity of knowing
this season of darkness will soon become light.

Senior Moments

You cannot place her name, her face
from just last week or long ago, when now
was mixed with hope and not the past.

You do not know if your aching rib
is just a recent but forgotten bruise
or a return of the cancer cut out years ago.

You do not know if your heart will last the night
or stop at three-billion beats since you were born
before the start of the Second World War.

But you know that light will appear at half past six,
the freight will rumble at dawn through the fields,
the lilacs bloom purple, the redbuds in pink.

The magpies will call from your backyard trees,
an Eastern aroma will arise from your tea,
and chances are you'll have twenty more years.

Old Guys

When MH commanded the second battalion, they charged
up mountains with bayonets drawn, pushed Nazi soldiers
over the Po, turned the tide of World War II. A former
sex biology prof, his lectures were always packed, and still
he writes hilarious poems for open mics. Widowed, now
one hundred, his mind remains sharp, his memories strong.

Nearing eighty with honors galore, EM is tops in his geology
field: plate tectonics and sites both earthly and astronomical.
A Renaissance man who played third cello in our university's
orchestra, he once performed Bach's *Prelude from Suite 2*
on a Nussbaum Travielo at the Cyprus shore, the very site
where Venus ascended full bloom. Often he fills our fading
minds too full, always inspires us to learn more.

A World War II army officer, RC survived Nazi gunners
at the Battle of the Bulge, earned the Silver Star, yet never
told us this story before he died. A former newspaper science
editor, his forte was writing insightful poems we took turns
reading aloud at his life celebration.

A physicist revered worldwide, JJ was there at the dawn
of the nuclear age. With eyes wide open against regulations,
he witnessed the blast of the first atomic bomb at 5:29 AM
on July 16, 1945. Seventy years later, he died of leukemia.
His memorial service was standing room only.

Once a physical therapist, KR, a past poet laureate of another
town, knows something and more about all there is to know.
He sparks our discussions with insightful ideas
he insists are merely suggestions.

A World War II navy veteran, respected attorney, CN's forte
was defending prison inmates. Broad-ranged in opinions, he
often proffered his legal views on the state of our troubled
world. Five years ago, he and his wife were murdered in bed
by a screwed-up high-school kid.

A college track quarter-miler, former state toxicologist, SD,
a recent widower, lives alone in the elder community he
and his wife helped to found. Now his flat feels empty of
of familiar sounds. Our meetings remain his fortnightly treasure.

A retired minister, college professor, WH spoke of his seminary
days, befriending the Rev. Dr. Martin Luther King, Jr. long before
the civil rights era. He spoke out when the Ku Klux Klan threatened
interracial friendships in his Kansas town. At age ninety-five,
a model for our lives, he accepted aging's relentless flow, simply
passed on. How we miss his inspiring kindness and wisdom.

An East Coast engineer who once built bridges near his Buffalo
hometown, PW has something to say about almost all there is
to know. As co-chair of our church's committee on sanctuary,
he stays up to speed on daily events and calamities.

As a teenager, I led a pack train in the Sierra Nevada, then spent
my twenty-first summer on a motorbike in Europe. Years later,
I rode an Arabian horse past the Egyptian pyramids, sprinkled
the ashes of my second-born son in the Thames at Cleopatra's
Needle, and practiced academic medicine for fifty years while
researching alcoholic liver disease, all fodder for my poetry career.

Grandad's Last Hike

I ascend the granite trail, step by cautious step,
climb the gravelly path around a narrow bend.
The mountain rises steeply on my right,
a precipice falls sharply off on my left,

The tops of fir trees loom below. I contemplate
oblivion. I'm the Grandad and Dad,
reliving the family hike, last climbed
when I was half my age.

My kids were then in their teens,
as theirs have now become,
far ahead at the top of the trail.
I'm sweat-soaked with fear.

My wavering feet seek solid anchor,
any perch on the sloping rock trail.
Hunched over quavering walking poles,
I'm consumed by mounting panic.

One slip on the gravel, anchored no more,
I'd plummet head first through the trees.
My skin would shred, arms and legs would break,
my skull would crack like an egg, my brain

become a mushy stain, oozing across the forest
floor. A firm and steady hand grasps my downhill
shoulder. The voice of my first-born son breaks
through my terror: "Dad, you OK?"

Breaking Eighty

At seventy-eight, I ran up granite stairs in a violent East Coast summer rainstorm, tripped, crashed forward head first, and bled profusely from a long gash in my forehead. After a wailing ambulance ride to the nearest ER, a young woman doc stitched me up, my attentive teenage granddaughter at my side. Once seen in the clinic back home, I learned that my head MRI was OK, while cognition tests showed minimal change. I'd entered the realm of the aged.

At seventy-nine on a family climb, I stood on a ledge looking down hundreds of feet through tops of towering pines. I imagined a fall that would break arms and legs on branches, splatter my brains across the forest floor. As I wobbled over walking poles in mounting panic, my elder son grasped my outside arm, asked "Dad, you OK?", and led me past my certain demise.

When I'd turned eighty, my college-aged granddaughter asked, "Grandad, how did you design your experiments?" Enchanted, I led her through the scientific method, second nature in my former career. My grandson, a tireless teenage athlete, chimed in: "Grandad, what was your best time in the two-mile run?" I replied, "Ten minutes, twenty-eight seconds in my last freshman track meet," adding that my alumnus donation requests always begin: "Dear student athlete." Eighty did not seem so old when my grandson replied: "Awesome time, Grandad!"

slanting sun
on golden oak leaves—
crickets singing

INTO THE NIGHT

Elegy for Ma

You married our Pa when twenty-three,
gave birth to four children over eight years.
When Pa was gone in the war, '42 to '45,
you held each of us close, as much as yourself,

comforted us all when air raid sirens whooped.
We lived in Dedham, five miles from the coast.
You kept goats for milk and a hen house for eggs,
raked chicken manure into our victory garden.

When a hen stopped laying eggs, you chopped off
its head, boiled the rest to be sure we had plenty to eat.
On victory day in '45, you took us down to the square,
made sure each had a turn on the church bell rope.

Fifteen years later, divorced, you directed
the Boston program for guests of State,
made lifelong friendships with foreign visitors,
invited many to stay at your home.

When you came to visit my family in Cairo
on your way to see new African friends,
you were amazed when a belly dancer
wrapped her silk scarf around my neck.

In your late sixties you took traffic control into your hands,
convinced Cambridge officials to close Sunday's flow,
created Riverbend Park across from your house.
A stone bench memorial honors your name.

In your eighties you wrote *The Claiming of the Shoe*,
a drama composed entirely of Shakespearean quotes,
and published *The Aunts*, a biography about the unusual
lives of your mother's four maiden sisters.

At aged ninety-nine on your deathbed, surrounded
by all four adult children, you asked my older brother
"Am I one hundred?" "Not yet," he said,
"still five months to go." "Good enough," you replied.

You drifted down your beloved Charles River,
miles downstream from our wartime home, entered
Boston harbor where your ancestors first landed,
became one with eternal waves washing the shore.

Spirits in the Ceiling

"Martha! We were pals long before your fame.
How I wish my beaux had been like yours!"
"Hallucinating?" I ask the hospice nurse.
"Is this the last stage of dying?"

"No," she says, "they're her long-lost friends
returned to dance in the ceiling. She's getting
ready to go to their eternal party in that space
between the stars and all the molecules of life."

A small cardboard box holds
gray ash and tiny white pieces
of her hundred-year-old bones,
gritty but easy to sift through our fingers.

We mix her remains with the soil
of a brittle young quince with orange buds
far above the blue-green sea and granite shore,

where gulls and breaking spray flash white in the sun,
the never-ceasing to and fro of crashing waves,
the constant refrain of her world.

We water the quince before walking away.

Into the Boston Night

The first of his wives, the last of his lovers,
all four of his offspring surrounded his bed
in the storied hospital where he'd learned his craft
more than fifty years before.

When I reached for his hand, his empty gaze
passed through the window, cracked open
to the last of winter's cold. His breath cycled
fast and shallow, then slow and deep,
sure signs his life would soon be done.

As a child I'd huddled freezing in his car
while he disappeared behind front doors
to bring his skills and hope to the sick within.
They paid for his care with eggs or freshly
baked bread in those late depression years.

In my teens, he told me stories of caring
for battle-worn soldiers in World War II.
I felt his excitement when he described
his research discoveries at the medical school
where he taught and practiced his skills.

His pulse quickened as he sat bolt upright.
His unfixed gaze swept over the room as if we
were mere strangers. Then he collapsed
onto his bed, returned to his final journey.

His breathing came relentlessly shallow; his pulse
slowed, then ceased. As his face turned to stone,
I felt a soft breeze float through the window
and into the Boston night, where snow
melted in rivulets, spring not far behind.

Forgiven

Now you're somewhere in space with the stars
or else on the crests of eternal waves.
Barely responsive on your deathbed day,
you never heard what I forgot to say.

Something about our childhoods together,
you ten, me seven, when you stole
my brand-new Lionel train and traded
it with your friend across the fence

for a set of English soldiers, later
rewarded to me by our referee mother.
Somehow fraternal betrayal faded away in the ether
of each of us growing up. You never said sorry,

I never forgave, and within my deepest memory
I mourned my lost train that was never returned.
What can I say today, seventy-four years later?
Shall I assume that in death's penumbra

you can sense my grief, feel my sorrow,
my wish to tell you that all childhood intrusions
were erased by later times together, when you
were always there for me, my big brother?

My Brother Lies in the Waves

When we were small boys, we would lie awake
by the gleam of the waxing gibbous moon
bathing the woods and our room in pallid light
down to the shore, across the nearby sea.

He knew how to tell when the tide was high
by the sound of crashing waves, the height
of their spray on the rocky shore, or low
when receding through tumbling pebbles,
pulling them out across the sand.

A foghorn groan from the horizon lighthouse
meant beware. Eight decades gone, he was taken away.
A monstrous wave crashed through his room,
pulled him out to sea, dragging last pebbles
of life behind. The foghorn groaned. I was alone.

ACKNOWLEDGMENTS

The author gratefully acknowledges the publications in which poems in this book first appeared:

Blood and Bourbon: "Bourbon Street Awakening"
Blood and Thunder: "Quality of Life"
Chest: "Tattoos"
Clerestory: "Upside Down"
Contemporary Haibun Online: "The Handout"
Contemporatry Poetry IV: "Senior Moments"
Degenerates: "Driving the Homeless," "Homeless Shelter," "Torn Fabric,"
    "Victims Remain in Our Prayers"
Edify Fiction: "Fault-Line Fury," "Forgiven"
Entering: Davis Poetry Anthology: "Winter Landscapes"
The Ghazal Page: "Forget-Me-Nots"
Haibun Today: "Breaking Eighty"
Hektoen International: "Informed Consent," "Letter to Pa," "Redemption,"
    "Tales Out of Medical School"
Journal of Modern Poetry: "I, Telemachus," "Mouth to Mouth"
Killjoy: "Feather River"
Medical Literary Messenger: "Mouth to Mouth"
Medusa's Kitchen: "The Odyssey of Retirement," "True Love"
The Moon: "Hopi Dancers," "Navajo Medicine"
Poetry Box: "Song of the Steelhead"
Poetry Now: "Magpies in Ascendance," "Waking Rituals," "The Watch Fixer"
Poetry Soup: "Saturday Farmers' Market"
Rosette Malificarum: "The Monster of Darkness," "Voice from the Grave of
    Reverend Reeb"
River Poets Journal: "Melting Pot"
The Sigh Press: "Legacies"
The Sirens Call: "Bombs in the Night"
Sisyphus: "Initiation Night"
Snapdragon: A Journal of Art & Healing: "Bucket of Blood," "Spirits in the
    Ceiling"
Tule Review: "Evolution Valley"
The Turnip Truck(s): "Grandma's Corpse"
Wood Coin: "In the Footsteps of the Parisian Poet"
Words Apart: "Extenuating Circumstances"

Yolo Crow: "In the Canyon," "Pacific Daybreak," "Rainbow Ride," "Return of the Magpies," "Standing in the Stream," "Twelve-Step Dante"

"Bombs in the Night" was among the Laureates' Choice winners in the 2017 Great River Shakespeare Festival's Maria W. Faust Sonnet Contest.

HOW I CAME TO WRITE POETRY

My first exposure to painstaking writing occurred in my psychiatry course during my second year in medical school, where I learned how to obtain and record a medical history—the basis of all medical practice. These intense interactions introduced me to the essentials of careful observation in evaluating patients who have been influenced by many human interactions and life events as well as by the causes and results of their illness.

As a medical resident, I was fortunate to have Dr. John Harris, a highly regarded academic physician, as my first mentor. He guided me through the processes of developing scientific hypotheses and clinical research plans and rigorously observing, collecting, and reporting clinical and scientific facts. My first published paper required at least ten revisions before it was accepted by an esteemed medical journal.

My academic medical career at the University of California Davis School of Medicine involved caring for patients, educating medical students, conducting scientific research, and writing a continuous stream of grant applications and articles for peer-reviewed journals. I received continuous funding for my basic and clinical research, spent ten years as editor for the leading scientific journal in my field, and published 105 original research articles and 110 book chapters, review articles, and editorials.

As retirement from medicine loomed, I realized I must develop a new career and began to take poetry courses offered by the Davis Arts Center, where Hannah Stein was my first teacher. In 2014, I learned that my alma mater Stanford University offers many online continuing education courses and have since completed ten poetry writing classes. I have also attended the Poetry Workshop (2018), the Society of the Muse of the Southwest Taos Writers Conference (2018 and 2019), and the Catamaran Writing Conference (2019). My first chapbook, *Breaking Eighty*, was published by Finishing Line Press. The present book is my first full-length poetry collection.

CPSIA information can be obtained
at www.ICGtesting.com
Printed in the USA
FSHW021633051019
62683FS

9 781646 620425